Blue Parrot

Peter Leigh

Published in association with
The Basic Skills Agency

WITHDRAWN

Hodder Murray

Orders: please contact Bookpoint Ltd, 130 Milton Park, Abingdon, Oxon OX14 4SB.
Telephone: (44) 01235 827720. Fax: (44) 01235 400454. Lines are open 9.00–6.00,
Monday to Saturday, with a 24-hour message answering service. Visit our website at
www.hoddereducation.co.uk

© Peter Leigh 2005
First published in 2005 by
Hodder Murray, a member of the Hodder Headline Group
338 Euston Road
London NW1 3BH

Impression number 10 9 8 7 6 5 4 3 2 1
Year   2010 2009 2008 2007 2006 2005

Cover illustration by Mark Preston/The Organisation
Illustrations by Pulsar Studio/Beehive Illustration
Typeset by Transet Limited, Coventry, England.
Printed in Great Britain by Athenaeum Press Ltd, Gateshead, Tyne & Wear.

A catalogue record for this title is available from the British Library

ISBN-10 0 340 90059 8
ISBN-13 9 780340 900598

About the Play

The People

- Rik
- Gary } two boys
- Jez
- Sam } two girls

The Scene

It is night-time in town.
There's a queue outside a club – The Blue Parrot.

Jez *and* **Sam** *are in the queue,*
Rik *and* **Gary** *come in, and join the end of it.*

Rik	Is this it, then?
Gary	Yes.
Rik	Are you sure?
Gary	Course I'm sure.
Rik	I don't want to go
	to the wrong place.
Gary	It's not the wrong place.
Rik	That's what you said last time –
	when we went to that rave.
	'I know the way,' you said.
	'I know how to get there.'
	And where did we end up?
	In the middle of an empty field,
	in the pouring rain.
Gary	That wasn't my fault.
Rik	You said that last time as well.
Gary	Well, it wasn't.
	How could I know
	they'd changed the date?
Rik	You might have guessed
	when the crowd we were following
	turned out to be a herd of cows.

Gary	Well, this is the right place.
	Definitely the right place!
	It's on the sign – The Blue Parrot.
Rik	The Blue Parrot?
	What kind of a name is that?
Gary	What's wrong with it?
Rik	It's stupid.
	All parrots are blue.
Gary	No, they're not.
Rik	Yes, they are.
	It's like calling it
	The White Sheep,
	or The Stripey Zebra.
Gary	All right.
Rik	… or The Tall Giraffe,
	or The Swimming Fish,
	or …
Gary	ALL RIGHT! Stop moaning.
Rik	It's not like The Red Lion
	or The Green Monkey.
	Why can't we go there?

Gary	You know why we can't go there.
	We got thrown out of both places.
	And whose fault was that?
Rik	All right.
Gary	It is not all right.
	I was doing well with that girl.
	She was really nice –
	until you started.
Rik	It wasn't my fault.
Gary	Oh, it was her fault, was it?
	It was *her* fault
	you kept tickling her feet?
Rik	I wasn't tickling her feet.
	It was a misunderstanding.
Gary	That's not what she called it.
Rik	Look, my stud had fallen
	on to the floor.
	I was looking for it, that's all.
	And I accidentally brushed
	against her foot.
Gary	Accidentally?
Rik	Yes, accidentally!

Gary	Those bouncers didn't think so!
Rik	Well ...
Gary	And what about The Green Monkey? You got locked in the ladies' loo.
Rik	Well that wasn't my fault either. I went the wrong way in the dark.
Gary	You went the wrong way years ago!
Rik	Oh shut up about it, will you! What's it like, this Blue Parrot?
Gary	Why do you want to know? We won't be here long enough to find out.
Rik	Don't worry. You won't be thrown out. Just tell me what it's like.
Gary	Well ... I don't know because I've never been. But people say it's very smart, and very expensive.
Rik	Expensive?
Gary	It's all right – just buy one drink and make it last.

Rik	I don't like the sound of this. It sounds real posh.
Gary	It is. It's not for riff-raff like you.
Rik	What do you mean? I can do posh.
Gary	What's your idea of posh, then?
Rik	There's The Green Monkey.
Gary	Where you can see the sweat running down the walls!
Rik	It's warm, that's all.
Gary	There's one toilet for everyone, and it's bring your own paper! Or The Red Lion. I suppose you think that's posh.

Rik	Oh, never mind that now.
	Look there, in front.
Gary	Where?
Rik	There … Up there in the queue.
	See those two girls?
Gary	Oh yes. Do you think
	they're posh? …

A few places up the queue,
Sam *and* **Jez** *are talking.*

Sam	So, what's it like then,
	this Blue Parrot?
Jez	Five.
Sam	Five? What are you talking about?
	I'm asking you what it's like.
Jez	Six.
Sam	What do you mean?
Jez	I'm counting the number of times
	you've asked me that question
	in the last five minutes.
Sam	What? 'What's it like?'
Jez	Seven.
Sam	Well, I want to know.

Jez	And I've told you four times.
	I'm not telling you again.
Sam	I just want to get some idea of it
	before I go in.
	That's all.
Jez	All right, listen very carefully.
	This is the last time,
	the very last time. OK?
Sam	OK!
Jez	I've never been here,
	but everyone says it's really posh.
Sam	Really posh!
	I don't think I've been
	anywhere really posh … Jez?
Jez	What?
Sam	Are you nervous?
Jez	Nervous?
Sam	Going to a posh place like this.
	Does it make you nervous?
Jez	Well … a bit.

They giggle.

Sam	Jez?
Jez	What?
Sam	Do I look all right?
Jez	You look fine.
Sam	What about this green top?
	Is it posh enough?
Jez	You look fine, believe me.
Sam	I mean, I could have worn
	the red, like you,
	but then I would have had
	to have my hair up,
	because the red looks best
	with my hair up,
	but then I would have to have worn
	the really high heels
	to go with my hair up,
	and the only thing that goes
	with the really high heels
	are the pink trousers,
	and they don't go
	with the red top.
	So I didn't … I wore the green.

Jez	(*sighs*) Believe me, you look fine.
Sam	I mean, you go to all this trouble and half the time I don't think anyone notices. Why do we bother? (**Jez** *says nothing.*) Jez?
Jez	What?
Sam	Do you think anyone will talk to us?
Jez	What?
Sam	I mean, this is a really posh place. Supposing the girls are all stuck-up, and won't talk to us.
Jez	I didn't come here to talk to girls.
Sam	Don't leave me on my own.
Jez	It's all right, I won't. I just want to meet some nice boys, that's all.
Sam	What about those two back there in the queue? Don't look now! They're looking at us ... (*pause*) ... Are they still looking at us?

Jez How do I know?
I'm not looking at them.

Sam *half-turns,*
looks at the ground
as though she's dropped something,
and then glances backwards.
She turns round quickly.

Sam They're still looking at us.
Face the front.

Back to **Rik** *and* **Gary**.

Rik   I don't know. How do you tell?

Gary   They look nice.
                   I like the one in the red top.

Rik   Quick, turn around.
                   She's looking at us.
                   You don't want to look back.

Gary   Why not?

Rik   It makes you look too interested.

Gary   Well, I am interested.

Rik   Girls don't like that.
                   Girls like a man
                   who's cool and distant.

Gary   What makes you such an expert
                   on what girls like?

Rik   I know what girls like.
                   I've been around.

Gary   The floor of The Red Lion!
                   That's the only place
                   you've been around.

Rik	Listen, if you want that girl in the red top to like you, you just ask me. I know all the best lines.
Gary	What best lines? What are you talking about?
Rik	All the lines that girls can't resist. I know them all.
Gary	Like what, for example?
Rik	Like this. You just tell her this, and she'll be all over you, drooling over you.
Gary	Come on, then.
Rik	You get really close to her, and then you say, 'I must be in heaven. I'm standing next to an angel.'
Gary	Rik, tell me honestly. Have you ever actually said that to a girl?

Rik	No, I'm saving it up
	for the right moment.
Gary	Take my advice.
	There will never be a right moment
	for that.
Rik	Well, what about this one?
	This is one of the very best.
	The Traffic Warden.
	One hundred per cent success!
Gary	The Traffic Warden?
Rik	Yes. Do you want to hear it?
Gary	I can't wait.
Rik	Well, you go up to her,
	and say, very quietly,
	'You look like a parking ticket!'
Gary	What?
Rik	'You look like a parking ticket!'
	And she's all puzzled about it.
	Then you look deep into her eyes,
	and you say,
	'Because you have "fine"
	written all over you!'

Gary	That's it?
Rik	That's it.
Gary	The Traffic Warden?
Rik	Yes.
Gary	'Fine' all over you?
Rik	Yes.
Gary	Rik, you are such a sad man. Do you know that?
Rik	They work, believe me.
Gary	What was it, 'drooling all over you'? Puking all over you, more like!
Rik	Well, what about ...?
Gary	Quick, the queue's moving. We're going in.

The queue moves forward and everyone goes in.

Inside the club.
Jez *and* **Sam** *are sitting at a table.*

14

Jez	This is a nice place, isn't it?
Sam	Yes. Have you met anyone yet?
Jez	Give me a chance.
Sam	Well, I don't care.
	Any boy will do me.
Jez	What? Any boy?
Sam	That's right.
	I'm fed up of waiting for
	Mr Wonderful.
	From now on,
	it's the first boy that comes along.
	(*Pause*)
	As long as he's fit ...
Jez	... and good-looking,
Sam	... and has plenty of money.

They both laugh.

	... and doesn't talk about football!
Jez	Oh, I know, or cars!
	Why is it that men can only talk
	about football or cars?

Sam	Or how great they are?
Jez	Or what a good job they have?
Sam	And how much money they earn?
Jez	And how lucky we are
	to be talking to them?

They both laugh again.

	Do you remember those old guys?
Sam	What, at The Green Monkey?
Jez	With all the hair …
Sam	… and the gold chains?
Jez	And all those cheesy lines.
	Do you remember?
	One of them said
	I looked like a parking ticket,
	'cos I had 'fine'
	written all over me.
Sam	Eurgh … The other one said
	he must be in heaven
	because there was an angel
	right next to him.

Jez	Yuk! … And Emma said the ones at The Red Lion are even worse. She said she was talking to one, and his mate kept tickling her feet.
Sam	What?
Jez	It's true. She had to complain in the end, and they were both thrown out.
Sam	Serves them right. I hope no one's like that here.

Gary *and* **Rik** *walk in.*

	Look, it's those two boys again, the ones from the queue. What do you think?
Jez	I think they look nice.
Sam	They look a bit young. Do you think they're allowed out this late?
Jez	Don't be silly.

Sam	Quick, turn round.
	They're looking this way.
Jez	We keep doing this.
Sam	You don't want to be seen
	looking at a boy.
	It makes you seem too keen.
Jez	You're the one who's desperate.
	'Any boy will do me.'
	That's what you said.
Sam	Yes, but I don't want
	them to know that, do I?
	Are they still looking this way?
Jez	They're coming over.
Sam	Pretend you haven't noticed.

Over to **Gary** *and* **Rik**.

Gary	Look, there are those two girls.
Rik	What two girls?
Gary	The ones from the queue.
	They're sitting down over there.
	The one in red looks really nice.

Rik	I like the other one.
	Let's go over and say hello.
Gary	What? You can't just go over
	and say hello, just like that.
Rik	Why not?
Gary	Well … it's embarrassing.
Rik	No, it's not.
	We're just saying hello.
Gary	It's too obvious.
	It makes it look like
	we're trying to pick them up.
Rik	We *are* trying to pick them up.
Gary	Yes, but you don't want
	them to know that, do you?
Rik	Listen, Gary,
	and you might learn something
	about girls.
	Now, why do you think those
	girls are here?
Gary	Well, to meet boys, I suppose.
Rik	And why are we here?
Gary	To meet girls.

Rik   Exactly.
They know that,
and we know that.
So let's stop messing about,
and get on with it.

Gary   Wait! What about being cool?
That's what you said.

Rik   You have to be cool and interested
at the same time.
Now, are you ready?

Gary   No.

Rik	Why not?
Gary	I won't know what to say.
Rik	I've told you what to say.
	Try The Traffic Warden or …
Gary	I can't say that.
Rik	I'm not wasting any more time.
	I'm going to say hello
	whether you're ready or not.
	(*He walks over, followed by* **Gary**.)
	Hello, can we join you?
Jez	Yes, of course.
Rik	My name's Rik, and this is Gary.
Gary	Hello.
Jez	I'm Jez, and this is Sam.
Sam	Hello.
Rik	Well, this is a nice place, isn't it?
Sam	Look, before you start,
	there's one thing
	you should know.
Rik	Oh? What's that, then?
Sam	You mustn't talk about football.
Rik	Right.
Jez	… or cars …

Gary	That's two things.
Sam	… or what a great job you have …
Gary	Three.
Jez	… or how much money you have, or how wonderful you are.
Rik	Right, well, in the first place, we hate football. At least, Gary hates it because he's no good at it. People call him the wonder goalie. Every time he plays, they wonder why.
Gary	Oh, ha, ha! Very funny!
Rik	Next, I haven't got a car. But we do have lots of money. Although if we buy you a drink, we won't be eating for a week.
Sam	No, you're joking.
Gary	He's exaggerating – only till Friday!

Everyone laughs.

Rik	If we can't talk about those things, what shall we talk about?
Jez	Anything. Anything at all.
Gary	Anything?
Sam	Yes, you can talk about Hollywood ...
Jez	... Bollywood ...
Sam	... politics ...
Jez	... magic tricks ...
Sam	... Britney Spears ...
Jez	Hang on! I can't think of a rhyme for Britney Spears.
Rik	Wait a minute. I can do magic tricks. At least, I can do one.
Sam	What's that, then?
Rik	(*looks* **Sam** *deep in the eyes*) I can see right inside your mind. I know what you're thinking.
Sam	What? You can't do that!
Rik	Yes, I can.

Sam	So what am I thinking now, then?
Rik	What, right now?
Sam	Yes. Tell me what I'm thinking.
Rik	All right, then.
	You are thinking ...
	(*leans forward again*)
	... you are thinking ...
	that I can't tell
	what you're thinking.
Sam	Wha—?

Everyone laughs.

Rik	See, I was right, wasn't I?
Jez	(*to* **Gary**) Have *you* got secret powers?
Gary	What?
Jez	Can *you* tell what I'm thinking?
Gary	O ... oh ...
	(*he looks nervously at* **Rik**, *who nods encouragingly.*)
	Oh yes ... I can.
Jez	So what am I thinking?

Gary	You're thinking ... you're thinking (*takes a deep breath*) that you must be in heaven.
Jez	What?
Gary	That you must be in heaven, sitting next to an angel like me.
Jez	What???
Gary	I'm sorry. That came out wrong. I didn't mean it like that. What I meant was that you think ... you're a traffic warden!
Jez	What???
Gary	No, that's wrong, as well ... I meant ... I meant ...
Jez	(*kindly*) What are you trying to say?
Gary	I'm trying to say that ... that I'm not very good at this. Chat-up lines, I mean.
Jez	Well, that's all right, because I don't want any.
Gary	But I do, that's the point.

Jez	You don't.
	Boys think they have to use
	these stupid lines, but they don't.
Gary	But I do. You don't understand.
	I want the best chat-up line ever,
	because ... because ...
	I think you look really ... nice.

Silence

Jez	That's the best thing
	anyone's ever said to me.
Sam	I think that's beautiful.
Rik	(*very serious*) It is beautiful.
	There's only one thing
	in the world more beautiful.

Everyone looks at him.

Sam	What's that?
Rik	Another drink! What do you want?

Everyone laughs!